"My ambition is always to get better and better" - Lionel Messi

CONTENT TABLE

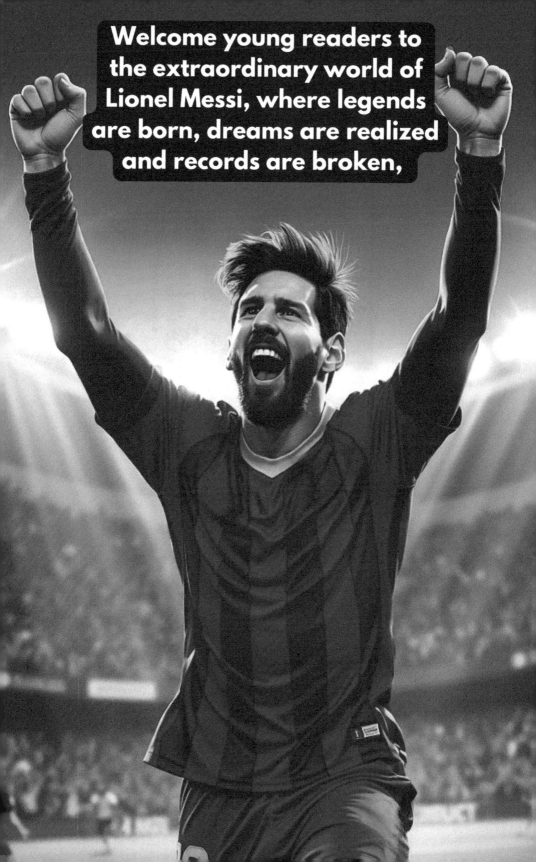

Welcome young readers to the extraordinary world of Lionel Messi, where legends are born, dreams are realized and records are broken,

CHAPTER 1
ORIGINS AND FIRST STEPS

Lionel Messi was born on 24 June 1987, in the sunny city of Rosario in Argentina, in a working class Italian family.

Where Messi's heart for the game was born was in an even tighter-knit community where some of the first kids played in his Rosario apartment block.

His father was Jorge, who worked in the town's steel factory; his mother Celia, who ran the house. They could afford little, but they encouraged their son's talent to flourish, recognising, from the moment he could walk, that the ball had chosen him.

As with many Argentine youngsters, Messi discovered his passion for football in the streets and on backyard grounds in his community.

However, even when he was a young player, his small stature was not glazed over when it came to the fact that he could control the ball in a brilliant and beautiful way.

At the age of six, Messi enrolled in a club called Grandoli which was near to his home, and where he began to be scouted. At this age, the youngster was already beginning to attract the attention of the press and to be compared to other Argentine footballers such as the legend Diego Maradona.

As his fame spread, interest from the professional clubs followed. At eight years of age, he was spotted by scouts of his club, Newell's Old Boys, Argentina's most renowned football academy.

He wanted to be a member of that team so much, that the rest of the family followed him to Rosario to start playing, too.

Finally with his talent Messi managed to get into one of the best academies for young soccer players in Argentina. This was a good opportunity for Messi to make a career in soccer.

Messi spent his formative years, both on and off the pitch, at Newell's. At the club's coaching centres, he continued to hone his technique and dribbling skills as well as his feel for the game. Messi stood out considerably from the rest of his teammates. Messi was undoubtedly Newell's most promising young player.

Despite being only 13 years old, Messi's performances for the youth teams made headlines, with many pundits and fans predicting a bright future for the boy. Many clubs such as Barcelona were interested in Messi.

But it wasn't all smooth sailing for Messi in his childhood either. At the age of 10, he was diagnosed with a growth hormone deficiency which threatened to derail his footballing ambitions. Messi's family decided to take the plunge, and sent him to Barcelona in Spain to receive the required medical treatment alongside the prospect of playing football.

Thus, at the tender age of 13 Messi signs for Barcelona Club, Messi turned his back on Argentina, and his footballing story has since unfurled as one of the greatest of the modern game.

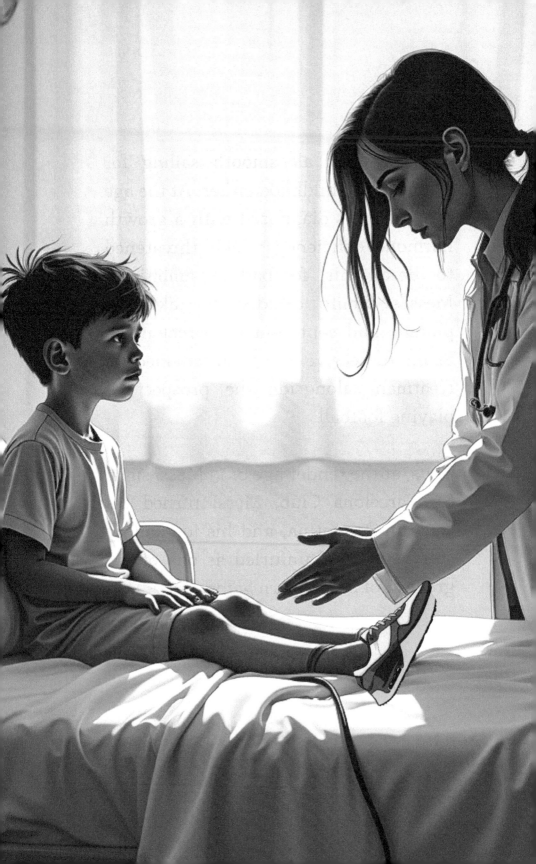

CHAPTER 2
THE MOVE TO BARCELONA

He left his hometown of Rosario behind, and headed towards the lights of Barcelona, Spain to begin his youth career at the infamous Club Barcelona youth academy, La Masia.

Lionel left the aiport in Barcelona and into the thrilling, foreign culture of Barcelona. Everything was new to him; the people, the language, the holed-out firmament, the maze of streets and the river humming through the city. Sure, he was nervous, but this was where he belonged – where he would finally be able to shed the skin he had been irritatingly stuck in, and blossom into the player he had always been dreaming of becoming.

For Lionel, competing with the other gifted preteens, teens and young men, most of whom had come to Barcelona from the corners of the globe, was a dream come true. Being part of La Masia meant being immersed in the club's unique soccer tradition, learning new techniques and skills that would propel him to the sport's highest level.

At La Masia, Messi worked hard every day. He was smaller than most of the other boys, but his skills with the ball made him stand out. Messi quickly impressed the coaches with his ability to dribble, pass, and score goals. He may have been quiet and shy off the field, but on the field, he was unstoppable.

While Messi emerged as a youth player for Barcelona, the coaches and players who watched him play from the junior ranks onwards agreed that he was a player with special qualities, his ability with the ball and his intuitive understanding of how to break down defences, dribble past opponents and create chances for his teammates unlike anything any of them had seen before.

Everything that he learned in his early years at Barcelona about overcoming obstacles, embracing adversity and the importance of faith will continue to serve him every day.

Messi's progress at La Masia was fast. As he grew stronger with the help of his treatment, his skills also continued to develop. His teammates and coaches knew that Messi had something truly special. His vision on the field, his ability to weave through defenders, and his incredible control of the ball were unlike anything they had seen before.

By the time Messi was 16, it was clear that he was ready for the next step. Barcelona's first team coaches began to notice him, and Messi started training with them. Although he was still a teenager, he was already playing like a professional soccer player.

CHAPTER 3
A rising star

In 2004, Messi made his debut for Barcelona's first team at just 17 years old! It was a dream come true for Messi, who had always wanted to play for the club. His first appearance was in a friendly match, and while he didn't score, everyone could see that this young player had something special.

Soon after, Messi played his first official match for Barcelona in La Liga, the top football league in Spain. He was the youngest player to wear the famous Barcelona jersey in a league match at the time. Messi didn't just make history with his debut—he showed glimpses of the magic that would make him a global star.

Not long after his debut, Messi scored his first goal for Barcelona in 2005. It was a moment he would never forget. The goal came after a brilliant pass from Ronaldinho, one of the best players in the world at the time and a mentor to young Messi. As Messi chipped the ball over the goalkeeper, the crowd roared with excitement, and his teammates celebrated with him. At that moment, it was clear that Messi was going to be a very special player.

Although Messi was young, his talent quickly earned him a spot in the first team. He was fast, clever, and had incredible control of the ball. He could dribble past defenders as if they weren't even there, and his vision on the field was unmatched.

His teammates and coaches believed in him, and Messi worked hard to keep improving. He trained every day, learning from experienced players like Ronaldinho and Samuel Eto'o. As Messi's confidence grew, so did his ability to make an impact in games. Even at a young age, Messi began to shine in big matches, helping Barcelona win important games.

As Messi continued to play more matches with the first team, his performances became more and more spectacular. He wasn't just scoring goals—he was creating moments of magic on the field. Messi's dribbling, speed, and creativity were unlike anything most people had seen before.

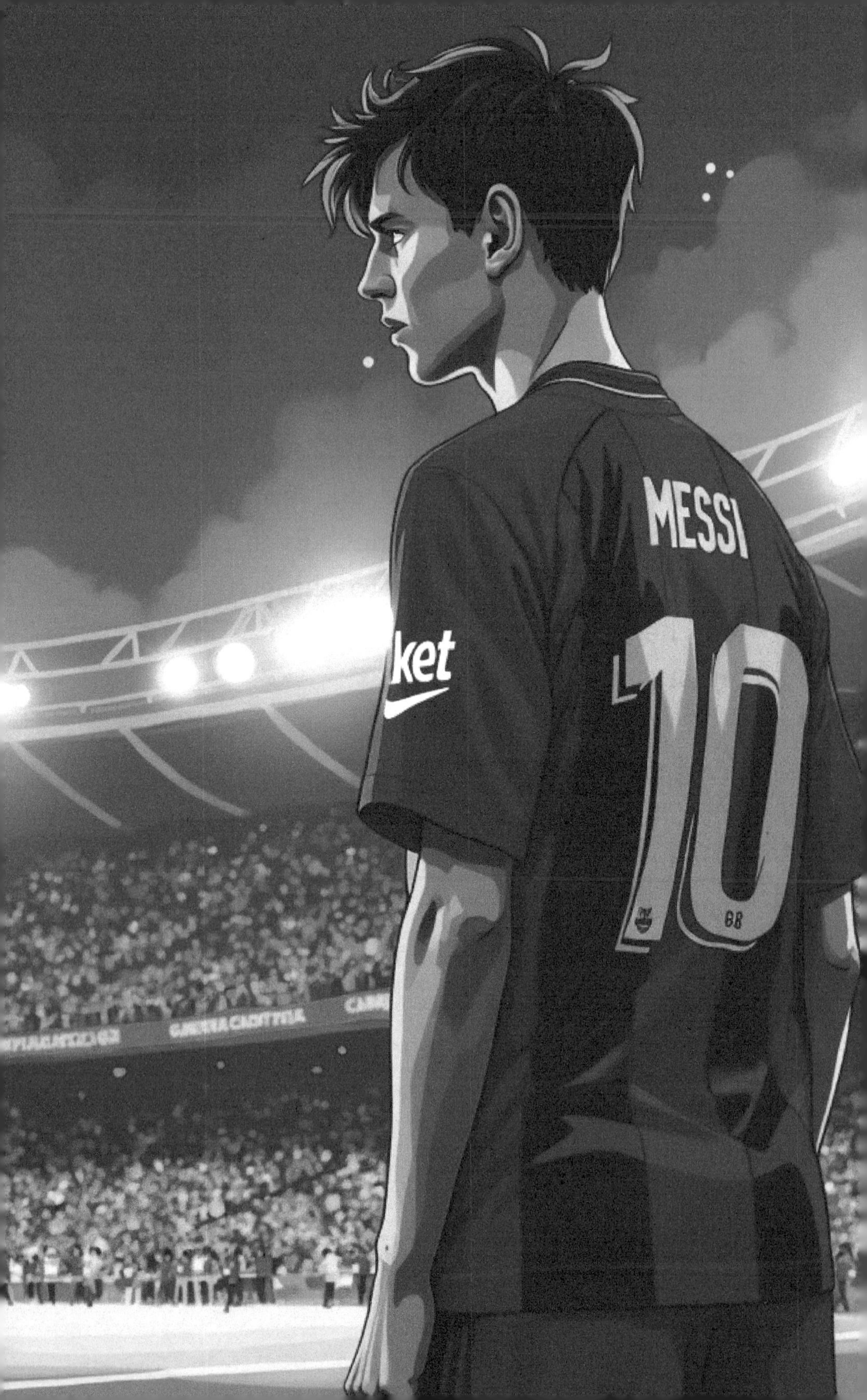
MESSI
10
ket

Messi's early years with Barcelona's first team were just the beginning of his legendary career. Even though he was still a teenager, Messi was already being compared to some of the greatest players in football history. But for Messi, it wasn't about the attention or the fame—it was about doing what he loved: playing football.

As he continued to grow and develop as a player, Messi's journey with Barcelona was only getting started. Little did anyone know, this quiet, humble boy from Argentina would go on to become one of the greatest players the world had ever seen.

CHAPTER 4
Achieving Greatness

After a few seasons at Barcelona, Lionel Messi became the heart of the team and one of the greatest players in the world. He helped Barcelona win 10 La Liga titles and 4 Champions League trophies. Every game, Messi amazed fans with his magical dribbles and incredible goals.

One of the most important periods in Messi's career was when Pep Guardiola became Barcelona's coach in 2008. Pep believed Messi was the key to making Barcelona the best team in the world. His tactics of fast passing and always attacking fit perfectly with Messi's style. They were able to win many championships and many people say this was the best football team ever.

Every game, Messi did something magical: he would dribble past defenders as if they weren't even there, and his shots were so precise that goalkeepers had no chance. Fans would hold their breath whenever Messi had the ball because they knew something amazing was about to happen. Season after season, he led FC Barcelona to one title and then another, racking up La Liga trophies, triumphs in the Copa del Rey, and Champions League crowns.

In 2009, Barcelona team, led by Messi, was the first club in the world to win the six titles played in the same season.

Messi was not alone in his successes. He played alongside some of the best players in the world, such as Andrés Iniesta, Xavi Hernández, and Gerard Piqué. These players formed a real family on the field. Xavi and Iniesta were masters with the ball in the midfield, always finding Messi with perfect passes. Together, they created brilliant plays that looked like something out of a video game.

Other very special teammates were Luis Suárez and Neymar. Messi, Suárez, and Neymar formed an incredibly famous attacking trio, known as 'MSN.' Together, they scored many goals and had fun both on and off the field

Messi's talent wasn't just recognized by fans, but by the entire world. He won the Ballon d'Or, the award for the best player in the world, a record 6 times while at Barcelona! This made Messi the most decorated player of his generation. But he wasn't alone in the spotlight. There was another player who was also fighting for the title of best in the world: Cristiano Ronaldo.

For years, Messi and Ronaldo competed at the highest level, each trying to outdo the other. Ronaldo, who played for Real Madrid, was strong, fast, and an incredible goal scorer. Their rivalry made every Barcelona vs. Real Madrid match even more exciting.

After 17 years of success at Barcelona, Messi had to leave in 2021. The club was facing financial problems and couldn't afford to keep him, even though Messi wanted to stay. It was a heartbreaking moment. Messi cried as he said goodbye to the club that had been his home since he was a boy.

Messi then joined Paris Saint-Germain (PSG), but his legacy at Barcelona will never be forgotten. With his 6 Ballon d'Ors, countless trophies, and legendary performances, Messi will always be remembered as the greatest player in Barcelona's history—and maybe in the history of football.

CHAPTER 5

Career
with Argentina

Even though Lionel Messi became a legend playing for Barcelona, his heart always belonged to his home country, Argentina. From a young age, Messi dreamed of wearing the blue and white jersey and winning trophies for his nation. His journey with Argentina was filled with excitement, challenges, and, in the end, great triumphs.

Messi began playing for Argentina at a very young age. By the time he was 18, he was already representing his country in the World Cup. All of Argentina was excited about Messi's incredible talent, and they hoped he could bring glory to the nation, just like Diego Maradona did in 1986. But winning a title with the national team wasn't easy for Messi.

For many years, Messi and Argentina came so close to winning important tournaments but fell just short. In 2014, they reached the final of the FIFA World Cup, but lost to Germany in extra time. Messi was heartbroken, as he desperately wanted to win the World Cup for his country.

Then, in the Copa América tournaments, Argentina lost in two finals, both times against Chile. Messi worked so hard and played his heart out, but the trophies kept slipping away. At one point, Messi was so disappointed that he even announced his retirement from international football in 2016, saying he couldn't take the heartbreak anymore. The whole country was in shock.

But Argentina wasn't ready to let Messi go. The fans, his teammates, and even the president of Argentina begged him to return. Messi, with his strong love for his country, decided to come back and fight for more titles.

In 2021, Messi's hard work and determination finally paid off. Argentina won the Copa América, defeating Brazil in the final. It was a historic victory because Argentina hadn't won a major international trophy in 28 years, and Messi was finally able to lift the trophy for his beloved country. The whole nation celebrated, and Messi's joy was clear as he held the Copa América trophy high in the air.

But the greatest triumph of all came in 2022. Messi led Argentina to victory in the FIFA World Cup in Qatar. After years of trying, Messi finally achieved his lifelong dream of winning the World Cup. Argentina defeated France in a dramatic final, and Messi was named the best player of the tournament. It was the perfect ending to his international career, and the entire world celebrated alongside him.

Messi's journey with Argentina wasn't always easy, but it showed how much he loved his country and how determined he was to bring joy to his people. . For his country and the world, Messi will always be remembered as one of the greatest footballers of all time.

CHAPTER 6

After Barcelona
(PSG and Inter Miami)

After many years playing for Barcelona, Lionel Messi had to say goodbye to the club in 2021. It was a very sad moment for him, as Barcelona had been his home since he was a boy. But even though his time at Barcelona ended, Messi was ready to start a new chapter in his career. His next stop: Paris Saint-Germain (PSG), one of the biggest teams in France.

When Messi arrived at PSG, the football world was buzzing with excitement. PSG already had an incredible squad, including Neymar, Messi's close friend and former teammate at Barcelona, and Kylian Mbappé, one of the most talented young players in the world. With these three superstars in the attack, fans expected something extraordinary.

In his first season at PSG, Messi helped the team win the Ligue 1 title, which is the top football league in France. Although adapting to a new country and a new team was challenging at times, Messi continued to showcase his magic on the pitch. His dribbling, vision, and passing remained world-class, and he created many memorable moments for fans.

Despite the domestic success, the one trophy PSG was desperate to win, the UEFA Champions League, remained out of reach. Even with Messi's brilliance, the team was knocked out before the final in both of his seasons. However, Messi's time in Paris reminded everyone that no matter where he plays, his skills, leadership, and love for the game are undeniable.

n 2023, Messi made a surprising decision. Instead of staying in Europe or returning to Barcelona, he announced he would be joining Inter Miami, a football team in the United States' Major League Soccer (MLS). This was a huge moment for soccer in the U.S., as Messi's arrival brought incredible excitement to the sport across the country.

Inter Miami was a young team that hadn't won many major trophies, but Messi saw it as an opportunity to take on a new challenge. He wanted to help grow soccer in the U.S. and bring his magic to a new part of the world. When Messi arrived in Miami, fans packed the stadiums to see him play. Every game felt like a special event, with people traveling from all over the country just to watch him in action.

When Messi joined Inter Miami, the team was struggling, sitting near the bottom of the league standings. But with Messi's leadership and brilliance on the field, things quickly changed. Messi led Inter Miami to win the Leagues Cup in 2023, the team's first major trophy in its history.

Messi's performances in the U.S. were nothing short of magical. His goals, assists, and incredible play brought joy to soccer fans all over the country, and he helped raise the profile of the MLS to a new level. Even people who didn't usually watch soccer started paying attention, because everyone wanted to see the legend that is Messi.

CHAPTER 7

Giving Back

One of the most important goals for Messi is to help children who are battling serious illnesses. Messi never forgot the help he received when he was younger and needed medical treatment for his growth condition. Now, he works to make sure that other kids, no matter where they are from, can get the care they need.

Messi's foundation has helped pay for treatments for children with cancer and other serious illnesses. In partnership with hospitals around the world, his foundation funds medical research and provides support for families who need help. Messi understands how important it is to give hope to kids who are sick and to let them know they are not alone in their fight.

In addition to helping with health, Messi also focuses on education and sports. He believes that every child should have the chance to go to school and play sports, just like he did when he was growing up. Messi's foundation has helped build classrooms, buy school supplies, and even create sports programs for kids who might not have access to them.

Messi understands how important football can be in shaping a child's future. That's why he works to make sure that children from poor communities can play the game they love. He knows that football teaches valuable lessons like teamwork, discipline, and perseverance..

Beyond his foundation, Messi is also a global ambassador for several important causes. He has worked with one of the most famous NGOs , the United Nations organization that helps children around the world, since 2010. As a Goodwill Ambassador, Messi has traveled to different countries to meet children and promote programs that protect their rights, especially those who are in vulnerable situations.

Messi uses his platform to raise awareness about issues like hunger, education, and health care, encouraging his millions of fans to get involved and make a difference. Even though he is one of the most famous athletes in the world, Messi always takes the time to show kindness to those who need it most.

Lionel Messi may be a football superstar, but his family is the most important part of his life. Messi is married to Antonela Roccuzzo, his childhood sweetheart from Rosario, Argentina. They've known each other since they were kids and got married in 2017. Antonela has always supported Messi throughout his career.

Together, Messi and Antonela have three sons: Thiago, Mateo, and Ciro. Messi loves spending time with his kids and often says that being a dad is one of the best things in his life. His family gives him strength, both on and off the field, and they are always cheering him on in everything he does.

So, this is the story of the world's greatest player of all time Lionel Messi. I hope you enjoyed it and I hope it encourage you to follow your dreams!

First paper book edition May 2024

Published by:

Dream Bigger Books

IMAGINE. EXPLORE.

SPECIAL BONUS

Want this bonus book for **FREE**?

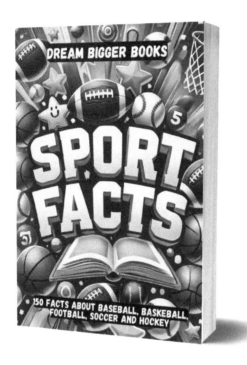

Get <u>**FREE**</u> unlimited access to it and all of our new books by joining our community!

Made in the USA
Coppell, TX
13 October 2024

38280589R00046